P

A Grading of the Human Species

A Grading of the Human Species

The following is a hypothetical Grading of how our Species is performing on Earth, now and throughout our entire existence. I (as a Human) will approach the Grading of our Species as from the perspective of the following Beings:

A highly successful Advanced Species living in another Galaxy far away from us. This Advanced Species has developed themselves into an A-type Advanced Species with the ability to watch other Worlds from far away for long periods of time. They have been watching us for a long time now and are ready to give their opinion and grade us on where our Species stands right now. They will use the same A, B, C, D, F grading system we use.

These far away Advanced A-type Beings are a little older than us and have been where we are going. They have also gone through the same Era's as us. The Industrial Era, The Technology Era, and the Information Era. We, as Humans, are currently within the Information Era and Technology Era.

"Is the Technology Era and Information Era strengthening or weakening Human Beings?" is an example of one of the questions that will be considered during this grading.

This is a critical time in any Advanced Species existence. This is where the A/B-type Advanced Species separates from the D/F-type Species. This is also the pivotal time where Humans either begin to flourish as an Advanced

Species or this is when they begin to crumble as an Advanced Species.

Very few species ever get to this level of development. Very few species ever get to this point in their existence; where they are at very high levels in Technology, Information and Communication. However, its what an Advanced Species DOES with all the Technology, all that Information, and all of the Communication capabilities that they possess. What and how an Advanced Species does with all of this decides the ultimate fate of that species. An Advanced Species that doesn't understand how to properly utilize the technology and information for the greater good of their species will eventually become a D/F-type species. Of course the opposite is true as well.

Which type of Advanced Species are Human Beings? Are they an A/B-type or D/F-type Advanced Species? Or are they just an average C-type Advanced Species? Keep reading to see how we graded them.

The following are the Categories that the Human Species will be graded on:

Category I: Technology
                - Inventions, Ease of life...etc

Category II: Economy
                - Money, jobs, perception of
                money and jobs...etc

Category III: Entertainment
- Music, tv, movies, art... etc

Category IV: Health
- Food, medicine, ability to heal ourselves or each other...etc

Category V: Management of Life's Stresses
- Does your species reduce or increase life's stresses on your Planet?

Category VI: Mental State
- Repetitive mistakes, species mental capacity and capabilities, open or close-minded, ability to change and adapt, ability to learn from the past ...etc

Category VII: Equality
- Acceptance of others and their differences, ability to work equally with others who are different...etc

Category VIII: Preparing the Young of your Species for Life's Challenges
- Parenting, mentoring, influencing, teaching, educating...etc

Category IX: Planet Maintenance
- Ability to clean up species-derived messes, ability to maintain your Planet, ability to recycle, repurpose and re-use, ability to control species-derived pollution levels...etc

Category I: Technology

Criteria for grading: What kind of innovations and inventions has your species created? Do those innovations and inventions reduce or increase the daily stresses of Human life? Has your species developed the ability to travel to and utilize other worlds within your Solar System/Galaxy?

Our Thoughts: Your Human species, for the most part, excels at this category. Your inventions are truly inspiring. From being able to communicate quickly and efficiently to nearly every corner of your Planet within a relatively short period of time should be commended. Your technology over the last decade (2010-2020) has exponentially grown into nearly all areas of your life. Some of your technologies are pointless and uninspired but much of that comes down to Human issues rather than technology. Same for your technology making your species' lives easier. Technology alone most likely does make many areas of your lives easier while some technology sets you back and makes life more difficult. However, its mostly not the technology thats the problem. Its how an Advanced Species utilizes that technology. But since this category is mostly based on the technological innovations without much emphasis on how they are used, our grading will be based more on what you created instead of how you are using it. What and how your species does with your technology will come out within the next several categories.

Your species does have some quite remarkable feats you should be proud of. Some with technology and a lot with the Human spirit along with your desire to explore the unknown. You guys excel at that aspect of your life on Planet Earth.

We are also impressed with how you figured out and mapped out much of the History of your Planet through the Geological Time Scale and your impressive work with the Fossil record.

Much of your medical technology is top notch as well. While most of your species fails to adequately treat chronic diseases, in our opinion, its not a technology or innovation problem.

NASA and Space Exploration entities like it are also some of your biggest achievements. We love the Hubble telescope. It gives your species and incredible eye, deep into the inner workings of our Universe. Then we were equally impressed with how you figured out how to fix the Hubble Telescope millions of miles away. Simply Brilliant!!

For all of these reasons, we give the Human species the following grade for Technology on your Planet.

Human Species Grade for Technology: A

Category II: Economy

<u>Criteria for grading:</u> Your species' ability to create a robust, dynamic economy that enhances the lives of the members of your species. Your species' ability to create jobs that not only provide consistently stable, secure lives but are also purpose driven. Is your species' perception of your Economy healthy or unhealthy, realistic or unrealistic?

<u>Our Thoughts:</u> This was a confusing one for us. Your species puts an ENORMOUS amount of emphasis on the importance of money and "The Economy". You would think that you would be "Masters" of creating and sustaining a stress-reducing economy. Its almost as if your species thinks this is the only thing that matters on Earth. The vast majority of your species puts money before anything and everything, including but not limited to, the health of your Planet, your own individual health, developing a problem-solving brain, your own offspring or anything that makes logical common-sense.

It gets even more confusing. Didn't your species create "The Economy"? Your economy was and is made by you and continued to be run by you. Then we ask this question? How are so few of your species benefiting from the very economy you created? How are people still starving, still homeless, still unequal in an economy you created?

As our species is, as every single species throughout the entire Universe is, we are all governed by the Natural Laws that developed over very long periods of time on our own respective Planets. For any Advanced Species to be an A/B-type species, they must work WITH the Natural Laws on their Planet, not AGAINST them. Successful Advanced Species do not create Non-Natural systems, like "The Economy", only to have them create more problems.

How do we know the economy is a Non-Natural system? How is the Country with one of the biggest economies $24 trillion in the negative? There are zero natural, real-living systems throughout the entire Universe that can function with a negative 24 trillion in anything.

Your Human economy is made-up and imaginary. No A/B-type Advanced Species would ever create a Non-Natural system, that they fully control and that continually holds back so many more than it helps. An Advanced Species is only as Great as a whole unit, not by a few individuals. Leaving so many of your species to struggle nearly every day of their lives because of something your species has created is disturbing and is vastly inhibiting your growth and development as an Advanced Species. This was a very hard thing for us to watch. So many good Humans (who could have made life on Planet Earth better) have been lost, neglected, cast-aside, hated, segregated, abused, and killed because of this one very small, man-made-up aspect of your existence on Planet Earth.

For all of these reasons, we give the Human species the following grade for The Economy on your Planet.

Human Species Grade for The Economy: F

Category III: Entertainment

Criteria for grading: Your species' ability to create a freely diverse depth of entertainment within music, tv, movies, art... etc. Are your forms of entertainment driven by the Human desire to "get better" or to "get richer"?

Our Thoughts: This one falls next in line, following your species emphasis on money. However, unlike money and the economy, relaxation and entertainment are natural parts of life for most species. Work hard, play hard as you say. Your species definitely has the "play hard" down.

Until we dug a little deeper. On the surface, it looks like your species has Mastered the ability of entertainment from sports, music, tv, and the arts. You have many diverse forms of entertainment. Many are simply brilliant and fantastically creative. At first anyway, then the simplistic realness of your self-made entertainment slowly starts to no longer feel so real anymore.

From movies, tv, music, sports, and everything in between, a familiar feeling of fake-ness moves in. When something starts to work and many of your species likes it, then the opportunity to make money moves in. It sure seems like your species thinks its too difficult to make money with too much freedom given to your artists. Much easier to streamline entertainment into narrow criteria sounding, looking, and feeling all the same. By taking away the freedom of your very own artists, creators, and entertainers for the sake of pumping out the same mindless crap over and over; you have virtually destroyed the ability for many in your species to freely create using their own unique gifts and own inner depth. The level and depth of your entertainment on Planet Earth is not even close to what it could or should be.

While your species has created some incredibly cool and unique forms of entertainment; the really good, real forms of Human entertainment are buried amongst the massive amount of superficial, soon-to-forget movies, songs, bands, art, etc. The vast majority of the entertainment your species' puts out lacks any kind of real emotional, connective depth. And when there is something that has depth and allows people to connect, its quickly and voraciously exploited for money and stripped down until its unrecognizable. Or maybe it is recognizable because it sounds, looks and feels like nearly everything else.

It gets better. Just when you finally do find some music, tv show, movie or some form of entertainment that allows you to dig deep into your thoughts and connect to things you haven't connected with before, a fucking advertisement always seems to find its way in. We should give your species' an F just for the exhaustive, obtrusive use of advertisements. Way too much!!

We ask this to you … Why is your species so fearful of feeling something real?

For all of these reasons, we give the Human species the following grade for Entertainment on your Planet.

Human Species Grade for Entertainment: D

Category IV: Health

<u>Criteria for grading:</u> Your species' ability to create medicines that enhance the health and longevity of its individuals. Your species' ability to heal oneself and each other. Your understanding and usage of food.

<u>Our Thoughts:</u> We first asked ourselves when thinking about how to grade you on this Category; how would an A-type Advanced Species perform in this Category? Well, since we are an A-type Advanced Species, we already knew what it took.

It took an enormous amount of open-mindedness and a variety of methods to eventually become consistently successful healers, especially of chronic diseases. Sticking to too few methods while judging, ridiculing, neglecting, or ignoring all other methods (even methods that work) will never get any Advanced Species to A/B levels.

First off, most of your species is exceptional at acute medical care (i.e. Emergency type trauma). You are pretty effective at fixing short-term health problems. However, your species starts to take a troubling turn when it comes to healing chronic diseases. Honestly, we feel like your species has created more chronic health problems than it has actually cured.

In some of your more "successful" modernized countries, 4 out of the top 5 causes of deaths are caused directly and indirectly by the very things that you have created. Accidents are usually the only top 5 cause of death not related to your species' actions. The other 4 are self-inflicted health-related problems, mostly heart related (heart attacks, strokes, aneurysms, etc). The other is cancer. Up to 90% of Cancer in your species is either created or made worse by the very environment that you have created. Cancer has been around for 100s of millions of years since cells have been dividing. But genetically-caused cancers are usually only around 10%

of any species, including the causes of most Modern cancers. Most of an Advanced Species cancers are not genetic-based, they are are environmentally-induced. Your species' high cancer rates (that are non-genetic) predictably follow certain modern lifestyles' "environments". The evidence is overwhelming. Change the environment, change the rate of cancer.

In short, by far and away, most of the deaths of your species are caused by the very lifestyle that you have created for yourself.

When it comes to food, your species can't seem to figure out how or what to do with it. There is so much inconsistent information on it. It is exhaustingly frustrating to listen to you and try to figure out how to eat healthy.

The following way of thinking allowed us to finally figure out foods' role in our species: Our species started thinking about how long we have been on our Planet. Then we started thinking about when we became an Advanced Species running and controlling our Planet, not just living on it. We have been on our Planet, much like your species, for several million years. We, also like you, have become a globally connected modernized species. We, like you, began altering our natural foods to more modernized convenient foods. We, like you, began to develop the same top 4 killers in our species.

So what's happening? No matter how untouchable you may seem as a young, naive newly Advanced Species, no species can ever get past the Natural Laws that were built into them and their Planet. The Laws of Nature have been set in place for billions and billions of years throughout the universe and into your Galaxy. To think that any species can arrogantly come along and change the billions-years-old Laws of Nature within a few hundred years is an absolute joke.

This is how we thought of food on our Planet and its relative importance to our existence... Most Advanced Species have been evolving and adapting to the environmental conditions on their Planet for millions of years before they even get to the point of having the chance to become an Advanced Species. Which means, they have been developing, evolving, and adapting along with whatever they can utilize for food in their environment. What do you think Humans ½ million, 1 million, or 2 million years ago were eating? Lots of different plants (fruits, nuts, seeds, veggies) and whatever animal or insect they could catch. And they most likely ate like this for 99.999% of their entire existence on Earth.

Its safe to say that for several million years the Human species has been eating, developing and evolving along with plants and animals that have also been evolving on Earth for millions of years. Its absurd to think that any species can alter food(diet) in just 150 years, to one that is so entirely different than their millions-of-years-old diet, to not expect long-term, chronic health problems. And that's exactly what happens every time. You can't drastically alter the millions-year-old Human diet and not expect life-debilitating and life-shortening health problems.

Hence, the top 4 out of 5 killers of modernized countries on your Planet Earth. You are up against 4 million year old Laws of Nature. Your entire existence, from every cell in your body to every chemical reaction within that cell has been built upon the Laws of Nature that have been fed into it for over 4 million years. We wish you the best of luck trying to maneuver around that.

Too few of your species get this for your species to excel at long-term health. The Human Species has arrogantly tried to circumvent very old built-in Laws of Food that your bodies, brains, and minds were built on. And to add further damage, most of the food you grow for yourself is further helping to make Planet Earth unhealthier. The Human Species is failing miserably at figuring this one out.

When we looked at your species' perspective on healing methods, you again came up short. It seems to be the theme so far with Humans, the physical aspects of what you do is usually of high quality while the mental aspects are not so.

Your species has a good variety of effective healing methods. You excel at that. If we were just grading on that, you would do well. However, as with most things, your mental-side to this was awful.

It was quite tiresome for us to watch your species continually discount healing methods that they did not agree with, even though they themselves had no experience with them. Modern Medical Doctors (Allopathic) look down upon natural healing methods. Naturalistic (Naturopathic)Doctors looked down upon Modern Medical Doctors. One group was against the other. One group would "Never Ever!" use the other group's methods, no matter what. So what do you end up with? Close-minded Doctors who only have a few tools in the medical tool-kit. You end up with Doctors who are quite limited in their healing methods. Thankfully you have Functional Doctors, Doctors who use all methods, methods that work. Natural first, drugs last. The Doctors/Healers that understand and work with the Humans' 4-million year old Immune System, along with the Humans' 4-million year old diet, along with using a wide variety of open-minded common-sense healing methods, from both Natural to Modern methods, are the true healers on Planet Earth. Unfortunately, we found very few Doctors/Healers who developed this unbiased, highly effective approach.

Unfortunately, the majority of your species does not believe in diversity of thought. So even though your species has invented, created, discovered many top-level medical achievements, your inability to diversify your mind-set around different healing methods sets you way back.

Then when we add in your inability to fully understand the importance of the Human Diet in relation to the entirety of your existence, your grade drops further.

We wondered how many modern medical Doctors would still be able to treat the Human body if their options for using modern drugs were taken away. What other treatment options have they been taught? If drugs become unavailable or ineffective, are modern Doctors on Earth properly prepared and educated enough to effectively treat and heal the Human body?

For all of these reasons, we give the Human species the following grade for Health on your Planet.

Human Species Grade for Health: D-

Category V: Management of Life's Stresses

Criteria for grading: Does your species reduce or increase life's stresses on your Planet? As your species progresses through time, does life get easier or harder? Is that because of something you have done or doing or are these stresses unrelated to your species actions?

Our Thoughts: We first asked ourselves which of life's stresses were brought on by the Human Species and which one's would still be there if Human's didn't exist.

For example, a meteor striking your Planet and causing a massive amount of chaos and stress would not be caused by Humans. Natural disasters fall under that category for this grading. Although the actions of any Advanced Species can alter the intensity and frequency of natural storms/disasters, we'll leave that out for now.

We were looking to observe the daily stress levels of the individuals of your species living under the life conditions that your species has set up. Your species has built your Economy, your Educational system, your Government, your Laws, your Cities, etc… If you are an A/B-type Advanced Species, we would expect to find low stress levels throughout your species, at least the modernized portion of your species.

We found quite the opposite in the Human Species. The vast majority of your species is currently and have been for awhile, living daily under very high stressful conditions. And the kicker is that your species has created nearly all of this stress. An A/B-type Advanced Species does not create a world that creates more stress than Natural life already brings. The main stress A/B-type Advanced Species undergo is from uncontrollable natural disasters. They have virtually eliminated species-created stresses from their daily lives. They finally decided to fix the fundamental problems that have chronically plagued their species. They have virtually eliminated suicide, poverty, homelessness, unemployment, starving, pollution, etc. They recognized this early enough to change, since most of their stresses were coming from the very systems they set up.

Your Human Species is quite the opposite with this one. Your arrogance doesn't allow you to see how ineffective the very systems you set up are. They are failing the majority of your species and you continually fail to recognize this.

The Economy that your species has created is not supporting enough of your people. Only a D/F-type species creates an economy where poverty, starvation, homelessness, and unemployment still exists. None of those should exist in a system that you created. Also, none of these are naturally created by the Planet you live on. This is all on you. Epic failure!

Stress for your species and most likely, most of all the other species on your Planet, are seeing a progressive increase in daily stress as you move into the year 2020. Humans live highly stressful lives. Humans live in increasingly highly stressful lives in the very environments they have created to reduce stress.

For all of these reasons, we give the Human species the following grade for Human management of life's stresses on your Planet.

Human Species Grade for Management of

Life's Stresses: F

Category VI: Mental State

Criteria for grading: Does your species make repetitive mistakes? Does your species learn from their History? What is your species mental capacity and capabilities? Open or close-minded, ability to change and adapt, ability to learn from the past?...etc

Our Thoughts: We wondered, if we took away the fancy new technology that came to each new generation of Humans, would we see similar patterns of fundamental behaviors? You bet we did. Humans have been acting the same since the beginning. The only difference now in 2020 is that your species has moved into rare territory. You have all the knowledge and technology you need to solve most of your current and past problems, excluding natural disasters beyond your control.

But the problem with your species is not what you can or cannot create. Your problem is your limited mental capacity. Humans are too arrogant and ignorant to see themselves as the problem-creators. Your mental perception of yourselves is fascinating. You are literally failing at realizing you are the problem. The excuses and blaming your species comes up with are entertaining to say the least.

Most Humans would rather do anything than stop and fix the basic, fundamental problems that have plagued your species since the beginning. We're guessing that fixing your own basic fundamental problems are not cool enough for you to worry about. So you continually "fix" surface issues while continually ignoring and neglecting the real problems.

Keep this in mind, we are grading your species as a whole. There are exceptions to some of these statements. There are a few individuals, a few countries, a few cultures who get this. But the few are too few to overcome the rest of your species.

An A/B-type Advanced Species who has decided to stop and fix their self-created fundamental problems is a species who gets to reap the benefits of that way of living. Everyone gets richer. No more poor, no more unemployed, no more starving, very little crime, more time off for play and creativity, more purposeful life work, more purposeful work, reduced stress, etc…

We finally got tired of daily struggles living on our Planet, much like many of your species who are exhausted with life on yours. There's no possible reason for an Advanced Species at your level of development to not be able to figure out a way to make a system, that you create, that lifts your species to higher levels, not the opposite.

When it comes to Humans being able to adapt to change, again we see poor mental capacity and capabilities. Human Beings are the worst species on Planet Earth right now when it comes to adapting to change. Your species is notorious for modifying the environment rather than adapting to it. This is one of those seemingly harmless short-term behaviors that can cause severe long-term problems.

Humans fail miserably at this. Its almost as if you have no long-term vision, purpose, or realistic perspective to what you are doing on Earth.

Your species ability to learn from the past is almost non-existent in the majority of your species. There is very little connection to what has happened to you species in the past to allow you to get to where you are. Humans have been making the same fundamental behavioral mistakes generation after generation for a very long time. They just get covered up by a new generation of arrogance bundled along with the new shiny technologies that each new generation creates. Add a little Smoke here… add some Mirrors over there. Lots of smoke and mirrors shadowing the real reasons for Human struggles.

Its quite easy to predict the long-term outcome of your species if you stay as you are. 50 years, 100 years, 1000, 10,000 years… doesn't matter. You will have the same exact problems you have now… inequality, hate, racism, poverty, pollution, unemployment, political corruption etc… Even if your species some how manages to "Conquer" Mars and establishes a new Human colony there, we're pretty sure you will bring the exact same problems there as you have here.

The Human species is encased in mental problems. Almost all of your problems on Earth right now are because of your mental state. An Advanced Species with a poor mental state may show these:

> … Inability to treat or see others as equals.
> …Too arrogant to see they are the cause of their problems.
> … Same fundamental problems never go away.
> … Create ineffective systems that create more unnecessary stress and more chronic problems.
> … Too many restrictive laws and rules.

For all of these reasons, we give the Human species the following grade for Mental State.

Human Species Grade for Mental State: F

Category VII: Equality

Criteria for grading: Your species' ability of accepting others who are different. Your species' ability to work with others. Your species' ability to work with others who are different. Your species' ability to treat all Humans as Equals.

Our Thoughts: If there is one fundamental quality that affects many, many other areas of an Advanced Species existence, this is it. If there is one category or fundamental behavioral quality that an Advanced Species should strive to excel at, its this one. This is the one a successful Advanced Species cannot neglect if they want to be an A/B-type species.

A globally connected species is immensely more powerful when its individual members are treated as Equals.

If Humans could Master this one aspect of life, they would be able to conquer anything. Treating others as equals and giving all Humans the same Human Rights is ABSOLUTELY ESSENTIAL if you want to become a dominant A/B Species. Everything else that you build and rebuild will eventually crumble if this one quality is not Mastered. This is it, this is the big one.

So how are Humans at this all-important trait? Well, to say the least, this very well may be your worse performance on this Grading Report. You guys are absolutely awful at this one. Some countries spend decades just to get to the point where women are allowed to vote. Still today in 2020, in some of the most progressive countries on Earth, females are being paid less for the same type and amount of work with the same background as males in the same position. Unacceptable for an Advanced Species.

There is so much hate on Planet Earth right now. There is so much separation between and within groups of people. From book clubs to hunting clubs, Humans from all over Earth trying to either one-up or ridicule or mock or gossip or isolate or control someone else in the group that doesn't do or see their way. Every where we looked, so many Humans are spending an exhaustive amount of their time on Earth trying to develop the image that they are better than others. Then parents do this in front of their kids and those kids become adults and they do it again in front of their kids...repeated generation after generation.

It seems to us that Humans either don't know how or don't think its important to treat others as Equals. You sure don't don't seem to be seeing the long-term damage that this type of behavior continuously causes.

Humans spend and exhaustive amount of their one life on Earth trying to gain pointless short-term "Wins". Most of these short-term "wins" that so many of your species craves and lives for come equipped with nasty, potentially damaging, "under-the-radar" long-term effects.

Many of these short-term "wins" are won by treating others as unequals. You may gain a "win" by pushing someone beneath you but the long-term wheels of chaos just started turning. No one can continually treat others as unequals and expect to have zero problems later on.

Inequality breeds an enormous amount of mental and behavioral problems in an Advanced Species like yourself.

Your Planet, because of your species, is inundated and infected at all levels with Inequality. Humans telling other Humans what and how to believe. Humans telling each other what and how to live their lives. Humans constantly shouting directions at each other… Do this that way! Do that this way!

Do you ever listen to the way your species talks to one another? Everybody is telling everybody what to do and most don't do any of it. So many of your species loves telling others what to do with their own lives. So many of your species thinks that they have the Right to tell others how to live their one life on Earth.

We were there too. We realized that not only it wasn't working, it was downright annoying for people to butt into other people's lives. We let our people live very free lives. We all have the same Equal Rights. We were tired of struggling with Inequality. Our species took off to much higher levels of living after just this one critical adjustment. We realized we were becoming an F-type species. We wanted more and better. We wanted to become more and better.

The amount of hate, racism, inequality, sexism, abuse, manipulation, etc. that is still present in your species today is absolutely ridiculous. It has gotten worse, not better, as Humans have moved through the most prosperous time in their existence.

For all of these reasons, we give the Human species the following grade for Equality.

Human Species Grade for Equality: F-

Category VIII: Preparing the Young of Your Species for Life's Challenges

- Parenting, mentoring, influencing, teaching, educating...etc

Criteria for grading: Human species' ability to develop problem-solving offspring. Human species' ability to prepare their young for life's challenges. Ability to allow your children to be able to develop within a more-free, less-restrictive environment.

Our Thoughts: We first asked ourselves what kind of kid would we be and what kind of adult would we become if we had to grow and develop under the same environmental conditions that adult Humans have created on Earth.

For example, some kids we watched had the following days more than they did not have them:

- Waking up in a <u>home</u> with parents who rarely try to work things out. Instead they wake up to highly-stressed parents that are consistently arguing. These consistently-arguing parents rarely have time to spend any real quality/productive time with their own offspring. Excuse after excuse... Blame after blame... neglect followed by more neglect.

- Then your kids go to <u>school</u>. There they find under- payed, under-appreciated, frustrated, highly stressed educators. These educators showcase more neglect. More passing the problem to the next person until the problem stops being a problem. Nothing real really ever gets solved. Swept under the rug comes to mind... Hence, real, worthwhile things rarely get accomplished.

- Then your kids are sent to the <u>school's counselor</u>. Guess what happens there. More unnecessary stress put on educators who are already under-appreciated and over-stressed. Then to pile on more insult to an already wide-open injury, more and more of your schools continually put

superficial data and testing over much-needed mental counseling and deep-connective learning.

- Even after school, more adult neglect on young Humans. "Adult needs" first followed by your "kids needs" when you have time to get to them (if you ever do)... is a reality we witnessed way too much.

- Your kids have very few places to go to get any real adult help. We have found very few adults that your kids should be looking up to and counting on.

We think we would become much like the kids you are producing today. We would not be able to solve our own problems. We would not be able to solve anybody else's problems. We would live in constant fear. The adults on Planet Earth are scared of so much and then they inject that fear into every new generation of kids.

We believe many Human adults create *more* problem-creating offspring than they do problem-solving ones.

We then asked this question about Human adults. What was their ability to allow their children to be able to develop within a more-free, less-restrictive environment? How much did Human adults *allow* versus *force,* the path of their kids? Were Human adults flexible and adaptable when it came down to allowing their kids to become who they wanted to be?

*Out of everything we watched over the many, many, many thousands of hours of observation of your species over the last few decades; this one, (**Parenting**) along with your species' inability to eliminate **Inequality**, are the two most important fundamental aspects of being a successful Advanced Species that you are continually and miserably failing at overcoming.*

Again, there is a small portion of your species that understands the fundamental importance of Equality and

Unbiased Teaching to their offspring; but again, for most of your species, a significant majority of your species is failing to realize the long-term set-backs you are setting up for yourselves when you continually fail to prioritize the importance of these.

Human adults tell their kids how and what to learn. They tell them how they should think about the information presented to them. Most don't give the information unbiasedly and allow for the child to make their own decision. Human adults deliver much self-biased information in favor of what the adult believes in, not whats factual or beneficial to the child. Most of them seem to be clueless to the long-term negative effects that this type of behavior can have on their own children.

Withholding information from your own kids as to get them to "see" your way on things can be quite damaging to the development of their brain. They will automatically be behind other kids who are raised by parents who are less restrictive and less biased in their approach to what's taught.

In short, the Human species is obsessed with barking out instructions to other people on how, when, and where to do or say anything. Your species is obsessed with telling others what to be, how to live, who to be, what to think, what to believe… etc. Its no different when it comes to your offspring. We feel that you care more about telling your kids what to do and who to be rather than allowing them to be what they want to be with their one life on Earth.

Yet another Human-offspring developmental problem: The practice of removing kids from their biological parents during the critical years of development sets up a very chaotic and problem-filled future in families and communities. Mothers, Fathers, and the Justice/Court/Custody System are setting up many future failures of many many Human offspring by continuing the practice of actively trying to keep biological parents out of their child's life. Your Human children have Human Rights too. Human offspring have a Right to physically, mentally, neurologically, behaviorally, epigenetically, and hormonally benefit from being able to develop along with their biological parents. That should not be taken away from them because their parents don't get along with each other or because the Court System is set up to separate kids from their parents. Why are some of your Justice Systems designed to punish the kids for what their parents are doing? We struggled with this one. (I go much deeper into this in Chapter 6 of Turtle)

Most of your offspring live and develop in very close-minded, restrictive, fearful, un-creative, and un-adaptable environments that Human adults have created. Nearly all of the problems that Human offspring have are caused by Human adults. Also, they are not adequately prepared for life's challenges.

For all of these reasons, we give the Human species the following grade for Preparing the Young of your Species for Life's Challenges.

Human Species Grade for Preparing
the Young of Your Species: F

Category IX: Planet Maintenance

Criteria for grading: Humans' ability to clean up their species-created messes. Ability to maintain, manage and clean Planet Earth. Your species' ability to recycle and reuse the things no longer used. Your ability to control species-created pollution. Your ability to work with and co-exist with the other species on your Planet...

Our Thoughts: I think most of you probably realize what your species' grade will be for this Category before even reading it. What is your Human ability to clean-up after yourself after making ecological messes (oil spills, elevated extinction rates, massive amounts of ever-growing Ocean-trash, non-recycled trash, air pollution, water pollution, soil pollution...etc)?

Not only does your species struggle at cleaning up its messes... to make it so much worse... Your species' still today, with all the current information and technology, does not connect the short-term dots with the long-term ones. You still make too many short-term decisions with too little thought to long-term outcome. There are ZERO A-type Advanced Species that do not clean-up and maintain its own Planet. They eventually learned that by consistently and continually maintaining and managing their Planet; it produced an enormous amount of long-term benefits. Once an Advanced Species figures out that working with Nature and the Natural Laws found on their Planet instead of against them; they find out that their Planet itself, will begin to heal itself.

Think of it like this. What would your Planet become if the Human Species were removed for 30-40 years? Would Planet Earth begin to crumble without you or would it begin to heal and rebuild without you? Since removal is not an option, A-type Advanced Species eventually choose to work with their Planet and let their Planet heal and rebuild itself as much as it can. Then the A-type species supplements and helps its

Planet where it needs it using the knowledge and technology that they have been creating.

We believe Planet Earth and most of its species would benefit greatly if the Human Species was removed. However, there is the other. The other being we believe that Earth would become an unstoppable, ever-giving force of a Planet, depending on if Humans are able to figure out how to work with their Planet instead of against it.

Planet Earth is a top 10 Planet throughout the entire Universe. Not a top 10%, a top 10 overall. Its a rare perfect beauty. You, the Human Species, are also a rare Being. You, especially the Human brain inside your head, is of very rare incredible-ness. The Human Brain is, in our opinion, the most incredibly complex, all-powerful problem-solving living thing that we have ever come across throughout the entire Universe. Your Human brains are even more capable than our brains as an A-type Advanced Species. The only difference is that we use ours different. You neglect, abuse, take-for-granted, and rarely use yours. We train, educate, nurture, develop, love ours.

When it comes to recycling and re-using that have previously been used, you again have pockets of high abilities to be really good at this. But as a Global species, your recycling and re-using of previously used products is awful. Much of what is supposed to be recycled ends up as trash in Earth's Oceans. Many of your current practices are not thought-out and are unsustainable.

How much of your species' time will be spent on cleaning up just Earth's Oceans? A lot. How much time would have been spent on cleaning up the Oceans if, from the beginning, a clear, thought-out, common-sense plan was laid out? Not much at all.

The Human Species struggles in controlling their own self-induced pollution levels. Once again, its not because of technological or knowledge-based inadequacies, its because of the constant fighting and disagreeing amongst the members of your species. Your species talks a lot, but doesn't really accomplish much anymore.

How does your species work with the other species on your Planet? Well, in short, most of you don't. Most of your species seems to look down upon and disregard the other 99.999% of living things on your Planet. If you can't get something from them, then they are no need to you.

Your species fails to realize that your species is nothing and has nothing without all of the other life around you. Remove Humans, life on Earth thrives. Remove all other species besides Humans, Earth ends.

This goes beyond the physical abuse of your Planet. For all the extinctions, forest loss, ocean pollution, soil depletion, nothing is as dangerous and long-term damaging as the extraordinary amount of arrogance you have about yourself and your place on Earth.

We often wonder what would happen if the All-powerful Human Brain was unrestricted and unleashed while Planet Earth was running at near top health. We often wonder if you wonder the same thing?

For all of these reasons, we give the Human Species the following grade for Planet Maintenance.

Human Species Grade for

Planet Maintenance: F

Overall Grades and Final Thoughts

Category I: Technology..............................A

Category II: Economy................................F

Category III: Entertainment.........................D

Category IV: Health...................................D-

Category V: Management of Life's Stresses.......F

Category VI: Mental State...........................F

Category VII: Equality..................................F-

Category VIII: Preparing the young of your
                Species for Life's Challenges...........F

Category IX: Planet Maintenance.....................F

Overall Grade............................F

Final Thoughts:
Although we graded the Human species as an F-type
Advanced Species, there is much silver-lining to this. As bad
as this report seems, and it is, the Human species is not very
far away from being a dominant A-type Advanced Species.
We will leave you with a few suggestions to get from an F-
type to an A-type in **Part II**. We are curious to see what the
Human species is capable of when it figures out its current
place in the History of this Universe. We believe that you
have the capabilities to turn nearly everything around in a

decade or two once you are able to overcome your mental inadequacies.

Part II: (starts on next page)

- Offers suggestions and ideas to further advance the Human Species while improving, managing, and maintaining your Planet.

For more of an in-depth look at the Human Species, including our life-inhibiting faults and our extraordinary mental capabilities:

- Check out Chapter 5 in the book Turtle

Part II

A Human Species and Planet Earth Recovery Plan

Suggestions for a Human Species and Planet Earth Recovery Plan

The following is a hypothetical Human Species and Planet Earth Recovery Plan. I (as a Human) will approach this hypothetical recovery plan as from the perspective of the A-type highly successful Advanced Species (from another Galaxy far far away from us) who gave our Grading Report. These will be suggestions from them to us. Since they graded us as an F-type species, they are offering us insight on how to become an efficiently-adaptive, effectively productive, dominantly-intelligent A/B-type Advanced Species.

Reading the Human Species Grading Report before reading this would make this much more understandable.

First, let's compare the mentality of an A/B-type Advanced Species versus an D/F-type species. The world, your species' place in that world, and your species' overall success in that world (Your Solar System/Galaxy), ultimately comes down to your perspective of that world and your place in that world.

Your overall successes and failures as an Advanced Species boils down to being consistently good at only a few core fundamental qualities. One of those qualities is one's perspective of the physical/metaphysical world. Those Advanced Species that mainly focus and succeed on the physical while rarely focusing on the metaphysical, rarely consistently succeed on

anything meaningful. (Meta means beyond. Metaphysical means beyond the physical. Meaning meta is what drives the physical behind that which we are seeing).

The Human species is relatively good with the physical world. However, most long-term sustainable high-achieving success, comes down to being able to "Master" what's beyond the physical which we cannot see. To be highly successful is to see and understand the tiniest, most simplistic to the largest, most complex of mechanisms driving our physical world.

Ask yourself this. What do you see and think about when you look at a tree? Do you just see and think about the physical bark, the leaves, the branches? Most of the Human species doesn't seem to care to see beyond that... to see the metaphysical... to see beyond the physical.

If a highly-successful open-minded Human or, any highly-successful Advanced Species, is looking at the same tree as a not-so-successful Advanced Species is, this is what they are thinking: Even if they do not know the names of the trees or their parts or even if they do not know much about trees, they still think like this: They have learned over time to look beyond what their eyes's are seeing.

They begin to "see" with their brains whats deep inside of that tree giving life to that tree. They begin to visualize the veins within those leaves and within those branches. They begin to visualize fluid flowing through those veins within those leaves and deep within those branches. They "see" those veins bringing food from the soil into the roots of that tree through the veins deep into the tree. They see the nutrients in those veins being deposited into individual cells throughout the tree. Eventually they will begin to see how this one tree is living amongst and within a highly connective living web of life made up of countless transactions between it and others. Highly successful Beings look at people this way too.

To become a sustainable, highly successful Advanced Species is to be "Masters" of the Metaphysical.

The Greatest Human (top 10%) athletes, musicians, teachers, doctors, or just being a Human... etc. have all learned to become Masters of the Metaphysical. They have learned how to dominate the mental-side of things. **And that is where any successful Advanced Species must be. They must consistently and continually dominate the mental-side (metaphysical/gray areas) of life.**

This is where the Human species is really struggling. If the Human species figures out how to dominate the mental-side of their existence on Planet Earth, there is no limit to what they can achieve. Even though we graded Humans as an F-type species, we believe that with a few key mental and perspective adjustments, Humans can become a dominant problem-solving A/B-type Advanced Species within a decade or two. You have the physical skills and creativeness already ready to go. Master the mental-side of your species' existence on Earth and watch your chronic problems begin to disappear while life gets easier and better.

Before we get into the mental changes an Advanced Species can make, we need to make something clear. Your entire species does not have to make these mental changes for your entire species and Planet to achieve what it wants to achieve. If any Advanced Species is waiting for **Everyone** in their species to "jump on board" to achieve these high levels of existence, you will never get to where you want to be. You may never get everyone to agree to everything. Sometimes an Advanced Species has to leave some of those small/close-minded mentality types behind.

It benefits any individual, family, community, business, culture, country, to leave close-minded, unadaptable Humans behind. Everybody can make their own decisions, but when you are making long-term decisions for the health of an entire Advanced Species AND an entire Planet **Full of other species**; some rigid mentality-types need to be left behind.

Humans can no longer wait for adults to agree with each other on how to get things done. It takes your species decades to get anything worthwhile done.

With that being said, if you are an individual, a family, a business, a city, a country, etc, and you are tired of the Human species and the exhausting, unnecessary, highly stressful way of life that you have to live with everyday, there is good news. You can basically live life on Earth completely opposite than how Humans live and become quite successful.

To dominate the <u>Mental-side</u> of life on your Planet; become really consistently good at these simple, yet highly effective fundamental aspects of being an A-type Advanced Species.

1. **<u>Equality:</u>** We started off with the most important one. This is the one quality that is the most interconnected to the other qualities that Humans possess. Meaning, if one consistently fails at this one, it will, eventually without fail, cause problems in many and virtually all other aspects of your life. If one consistently succeeds at this one, chronic life problems will begin to disappear while the highly developed hidden gifts found deep within the Human brain begin to appear.

Guaranteed chronic problems will always show up when there is Inequality found in any Human relationship.

We can basically explain the Human species' past, present, and future failures and/or successes from only 4 little lines. Those *4 lines on the front cover of the book Turtle* (thoroughly explained in Chapter 5 Section 5.19-5.22) can and does explain nearly the entirety of the Human species on Earth.

The amount of time and energy Humans waste on trying to keep one another beneath them is astounding and exhausting. There are only a very few Humans that continually get this one right. The majority of Humans spend the majority of their one adult life on Earth trying anything they can do to try to keep others unequal to them.

This is a Fair Warning to Humans: You can "Master" every other aspect of living correctly on Planet Earth, then fail at this one aspect; then ultimately fail in the long-term as an Advanced Species. Simply put, if you fail at this one as an Advanced Species, you fail.

This is one of those traits that can bring an Advanced Species down the path leading towards extinction.

This is the one quality that other animals on your Planet cannot mentally overcome. But you can. An Advanced Species has to be able overcome species-wide inequality if it wants any chance in maximizing its potential.

2. Letting individual members of your species live free: Humans live daily life with an enormous amount rules and laws, which brings on more unnecessary Human-induced stress. The adults of the Human species are obsessed with controlling the lives of others. Too many laws, too many rules, too many restrictions on living a free-life. Humans who make all of these rules and laws continually fail to recognize that it is these very intrusive rules and laws that create unruly, predictably dangerous Human behavior.

Observe and learn for yourself. The evidence is everywhere all around you, if you just unbiasedly look. Whether it be families or countries or anything in-between, the worst behavior is seen where there are more restrictive laws and rules and where there is less personal freedom. There are reactions to actions.

So to be an A-type species or and an A-type individual, it saves a lot of time and energy to treat others as equals. It also builds up and deeply develops the Advanced Species' brain. One equal brain working with other equal brains creates much more intelligence in each of the individual brains. Instead of constantly trying to push others below us, we work with others to keep them equal to us. It goes the other way too. It doesn't work if the people you work with or have relationships with are trying to push you below them. You have to rise up against them and rise to their equal.

Unless they are asshole, self-centered Humans; then pass them up and don't look back.

Humans waste most of their time on Earth trying to control other peoples' lives. We wonder what Humans could become if they wouldn't waste their existence on the pointless obsession of trying to control others and the lives' of others.
It's as if very few Humans understand the long-term disastrous effects of the suffocating, unnecessary, mind-boggling made-up ignorant laws and rules that your species continually comes up with to live by. These suffocating, unnecessary, mind-boggling made-up ignorant laws and rules are found throughout individuals, families, businesses, cultures, cities, and countries. Fear of what "may" happen in the future drives most of these life-inhibiting rules and laws.

Being fearful of things that you shouldn't be fearful of brings about this devastatingly crippling Advanced Species trait.

We, as an A-type Advanced Species, decided to do the opposite. We gave our individual members the chance to make their own decisions regarding their own life. Since we, and you, have made it through the Information and Technology Era, we decided we wanted to see what would happen if we stopped coddling and assisting individual members of our species that resisted intellectual progressive, common-sense change.

There is a portion of all Advanced Species that may need to be <u>mentally</u> left behind to advance the rest of the species and to maintain and manage the Planet. These individuals choose their own perspective and the rest of our species respects that. **However, we will not hold an entire Advanced Species, a Planet, and an entire Solar System back; just because a group of close-minded individuals are unwilling to adapt to change.**

One would think, why would anyone want to hold back an Advanced Species from creating a highly efficient, equalized, productive, clean-living, ever-giving Planet? One would have to meet the Human Species on Earth.

3. Re-evaluating the Human Perception of their Place in the Universe and on their Planet:
The third mental aspect of life that Humans will need to improve in is this: Their Arrogance and Ignorance.

If any mental aspect, besides Inequality, can lead to the extinction of the Human Species, its these two, Arrogance and Ignorance.

"Ignorance is Bliss" helpfully describes many of the Human species. If you are too ignorant as to the harm you are causing to each other and to your one and only Planet, then you should also be ignorant to the fact that the Natural Laws of your Planet, your Solar System, and the billions of year-old Natural Laws of the Universe that came way before you, will eventually destroy your ignorant-ass species.

Humans' arrogance is yet another mental hurdle you will have to overcome to become a successful species. Too many Humans continually believe that they are so much more "special" than all other species on Earth. Too many Humans continually take from the non-human species while also continually taking from their own Planet; while not enough believe in giving back to either of them.

Also, Humans believe that they can somehow bypass the billions-of-year-old Laws of the Universe because of how "special" they feel about themselves. They basically think that they can alter anything they want and The Laws of Nature don't apply to them.

Again, once an Advanced Species overcomes these self-made perspectives of themselves, higher levels of development can then be reached.

We have found that most Human Beings we have observed fall into one of the following mentality types. However, one can change mentality types if one continually challenges their inner thoughts, beliefs and perspectives. If one challenges themselves enough, one can maneuver through each of the mentality types. This will give one a much greater depth of knowledge and understanding of Human life on Earth. Only a very few Humans, ever, have challenged themselves enough to adventure deep into the various mentality types. These Humans are the very essence of what the Human Being has the potential of becoming. Throughout the book <u>Turtle</u>, I refer to these Humans as "Highly Successful Humans".

<u>The 4 Mentality Types of the Human Species Found on Planet Earth:</u>

The following are flexible/fluid type percentages that can fluctuate depending on the individual, family, group, or culture of Humans one is talking about. Meaning, more successful or unsuccessful individuals/families/groups/cultures of Humans will have more or less of certain mentality types within them.

Before we get into the mentality types, there is variation within each mentality type. There are lower, middle, and higher levels of each Mentality type. The lowest levels of each mentality type is the least successful *within* that mentality type. The higher levels of each mentality type is the most successful *within* each mentality type.

The mentality type that is mostly likely to cross over and become a new, better mentality type are the ones currently in the higher levels of each mentality. The ones in the lowest levels of a particular mentality will struggle the most when trying to leave that particular mentality type. For example, the 40% mentality is the least successful Human mentality of all the types. *Keep reading for much more about this*. However, the higher levels of the 40% mentality are the ones that are the most likely and willing to **change** for the better and become other mentality types, just as the higher levels of the 50% and 2% mentality types would. The opposite is true as well, especially for the 40% mentality. The lower levels of the 40% mentality are almost impossible to work with. The possess the highly dangerous ability of not wanting change. Its a waste of time on Earth trying to convince this group of Humans of anything factual, helpful, or intelligent. They seem to only believe in one thing and never stray from that. *If you are trying to better yourself or your Planet, why waste your time and energy trying to convince Humans that can never be convinced. Leave them behind!*

Your species has already figured out something quite fascinating that really holds true here. Within the most basic, fundamentals of Psychology, there it is, right there for you to learn. Less than 10% of people <u>change</u> from their originally-developed mentality.

We think less than 10% of the Human species (throughout the entirety of their existence) challenged themselves enough to become something different than their original mentality.

From our many thousands and thousands and thousands of hours of unbiasedly observing the Human Species, we completely agree with that statement. We believe that somewhere between @ 90-98% (depending where you look) of the Human Species adults have the same mentality that they originally developed during the ages of 12 through 18. *Meaning, roughly up to @ 8% of all Human adults that have ever lived on Planet Earth, have* **challenged themselves** *enough to truly change their originally developed mentality and perspective of life.*

Most likely, whichever your personality type was in high-school, you still have. The people that controlled you and looked down on you in high-school, most likely are the same/similar types of adults that control/manipulate your life and look down on you now. The people that you controlled and looked down on as less-than you in high-school most likely are the same/similar types as you look down to and try to control/manipulate today.

We believe that less than 10% of Humans have found true freedom within themselves. Those are the ones that live and flourish with and within the Laws of Nature on Planet Earth... Definitely not against them. They have figured out how to release their minds and brains while freeing them from many Human-induced, made-up restrictions. These are the Humans who are not bound by unnecessary Human-made-up life rules. These are the Humans who have Mastered life on Earth, physically and mentally, the Physical and the Metaphysical. We believe they make up **@8% of Human Mentalities,** but they may make up much less than that in certain chronically struggling areas on Earth.

@ 8% Human's Mentality

→ Most productive and successful of the Humans.

→ Skilled and can work in a variety of areas. Highly successful in many different areas of life.

→ Continually work on building and strengthening their mind and brain.

→ Highly adaptable to change.

→ Wastes very little of their one time on Earth on time/energy wasting activities such as telling others what to do, gossiping, cheating, lying, jealousy, controlling, manipulating, abusing, neglecting others etc…

→ Spends more of their time living and learning as many different lives as they can while on Earth.

→ Blames themselves first.

→ Love to be challenged. Do not like taking the easy way out.

→ Have developed long-term vision. They learn and grow from their previous mistakes.

→ Allow themselves to make many mistakes when learning something new.

→ Believe that "The economy" is a small part of what life is about on Earth.

→ Produce much more than they talk.

→ Work exceptionally well with others who are different than them.

→ Are simply the most incredible parents we've ever observed. High degree of open-mindedness and adaptability. Their offspring developed into problem-solvers, not problem-creators.

→ Have Mastered the Physical AND the Metaphysical on Planet Earth.

The other 3 Mentality types:

@ 40% Humans' Mentality

→ Least productive and least successful of the Human mentality types.

→ Have developed a parasitic relationship with the 2% mentality.

→ Meaning that this mentality type tends to follow and depends heavily on the 2% mentality types' lead.

→ Tend to NOT see through the mask that their 2% leaders portray. Tend to back their 2% leaders in most situations, even if it causes more long-term damage to their own life.

→ Possess very few skills. Can basically only work in 1 or 2 types of jobs.

→ Most in this mentality type do not continually work on developing any old or new skills. They mostly never get better at their jobs, no matter how long they work there. Many don't see the long-term benefits of continually learning. Many stop learning after they get a job.

→ Dislikes most change. Has a very hard time adapting to most change. Often refuses to leave jobs or relationships that cause further long-term problems.

→ Often fails to see any connection between past, present, and future events.

→ Repeats the same mistakes over and over.

→ Most relationships have the same outcome.

→ Their offspring develop their lives around the same chronic mistakes and problems that their parents had.

→ Create offspring that tend to create more problems than they are able to solve.

→ Wastes virtually an entire lifetime waiting for someone or something else to make their lives better.

→ Wastes much of their one time on Earth on time/energy wasting activities like gossiping, cheating, lying, jealousy, controlling, manipulating, abusing, neglecting others etc…

→ Has little to no long-term vision.

→ Rarely works with others who are different than them.

→ Overwhelmingly blames others rather than themselves.

→ Tend to NOT follow the 50% mentality's advice.

→ Tend TO follow the 2% mentality's advice to fault.

→ This is the easiest mentality type to manipulate and control and sell meaningless shit to.

→ Tend to vote in high numbers because they believe in one, or a few people in high positions, fixing all of their life problems.

→ Live in the 10% "Black and White" Physical world. Fail to understand the 90% "Gray" Metaphysical world.

→ Are happier when getting paper degrees or bloated job Titles versus getting challenged.

→ Believe that "The economy", money, and jobs are the majority of what life on Earth should be about.

→ Talk way more than produce.

→ Fear of what "MAY" happen, Fear of different, Fear of this, Fear of that *dominates* this mentality.

Bottom Line on the 40% Human Mentality:

This mentality type is usually waiting for someone else or something else to do the real work for them to make their lives better. Many of them fail to realize that the very thing they are waiting for will never come. It will never come because they are waiting for someone else to do it for them. Good luck with that. We ask you to search throughout the History of your species and find examples where Humans have consistently and correctly done the right thing and made things easier and better for the majority of Humans.

If you have been developed in a 40% mentality environment, the good news is that you don't have to stay there. (*Chapters 1-4 explains how in the book Turtle*)

For me, as myself as a Human, I spent most of my life in the 40% mentality as I was developed in a 40% mentality environment. This is where I was the most miserable. This is where I was the most fearful of everything. This is where I routinely failed and rarely gained. My life was the same everyday. All of my relationships were the same. I was highly dependent on other people doing things for me. This is where I learned the least. This is where I was the most unintelligent. This is where I was the most ignorant and arrogant. This is where I was a problem-creator, not a problem-solver. This is where I was the most fake. This is where I was the most into my own selfish needs and wants. **This is where I was the least free…**

@ 50% Humans' Mentality

→ Mostly productive but possesses a low variety of skills.

→ Spends an enormous amount of time becoming skilled at very fews skills. Basically stuck in the one career they built for themselves.

→ Tend TO see through the Mask that their 2% leaders portray.

→ Tend NOT to back their 2% leaders in most situations. Tend to protest against their leaders.

→ Tend to be stuck between standing up to their Leaders and keeping their current situation. "Either shut up and keep your job or fight for what's Right and lose your job" can be found within this type.

→ Fear of what they "May become" or "What they may lose" dominates this mentality.

→ <u>Fear</u> of becoming poor, unpopular, single, divorced, unemployed, etc... confuses and mostly shuts-down the intelligent long-term decision-making this mentality-type possesses.

→ Protest about what they don't like more than they challenge their individual selves to change.

→ Like to give out advice that very few follow. 40% mentality types mostly follow the 2% mentality types advice and ignores the 50%. While the 50% mentality types somewhat follow the advice of other 50% mentality types. Simply put, many waste an enormous amount of time giving advice to the very few people who listen.

→ Mostly fail to connect with what they perceive as reality which is reality. Most are not listening to their own advice. Are you giving advice to satisfy your own needs or to help others? No one seems to be listening to anyone's advice, so why waste the time and energy?

Bottom Line on the 50% Human Mentality:

This mentality type is mostly dominated by the fear of becoming a less-than or losing what they perceive as being secure and successful. This is the mentality type that sees through the bullshit that their husband, wife, boss, and leaders are throwing at them. *However, this is also the mentality type that is too fearful of standing up to what is wrong so as to keep what is comfortable.*

For me, as myself as a Human, *(as a 50% mentality after growing and developing out of my 40% mentality)*; was more successful in my career and my life. I was also more confident in myself. However, I put too much time and energy into one type of career and neglected too many other areas of my life. When I wanted to stand up to my Employer because of unjust working conditions, I quickly realized two things. I can keep my seemingly comfortable life and keep my opinions to myself or I could stand up to what I believe is "Right" and potentially lose everything.

This is also the mentality where I began to believe I wasn't as free as I thought.

@2% of Humans' Mentality

→ The local, regional, national, and international Leaders of Earth.

→ ***Important:*** 2% Leaders can have have any of the other 3 mentality types, with the 8% Mentality-type leaders being the most successful. The leaders with the 40% mentality types are the least successful of the leaders.

→ Have developed a highly unproductive relationship with the 40% mentality.

→ Most start out with good intentions.

→ Unfortunately most fall into the very familiar but very much ignorantly ignored "Stanford Experiment" state of mind. Most Humans, throughout the History of their time on Earth, who have gained any kind of power have fell into the same trap of authoritarianism as most of you will eventually fall into.

→ Have good intentions until they get a little power. Then the same results as always... Do whatever you have to do to retain your position. Bend the legal laws, bend the ethical laws. Keep those below you, below you, no matter what.

→ Many 2% mentality types fail to recognize the uniqueness of their position. Many Human leaders follow the same predictable path of working above their workers instead of working with them. *8% leaders work as equals with the people beneath them, not as greater-thans.*

→ Any leader will gain immensely more in the long-term if that leader secures the fundamental basics of their people. Could you imagine what would happen to a leader if they solved/reduced poverty, homelessness, Human inequality, air pollution, water pollution, unemployment...etc...etc...etc...? **They would get re-elected and praised as a fucking savior!!!** Yet so few take this path...

→ **Talk way more more than produce!** Many in this mentality type get into their positions because of their ability to talk rather than solve problems. More smoke and mirrors.

→ The opposite to this is when an **8%** mentality type becomes a Leader. An **8%** Mentality Leader is the best problem-solver, the most adaptable, the most efficient, and the most complete out of all the Human Leaders. Unfortunately these types of leaders are exceedingly rare.

Bottom Line on the 2% Human Mentality:

This mentality type has an interesting position. You have either been born into, elected into, hired, or chosen for your position.

We ask this question, what would your leaders become if they didn't follow the predictable Human behavior seen in the Stanford Experiment? What would your leaders become if they actually solved real problems rather than turning into the predictable authoritarians the guards turned into after a very short period of time (days)?

If your leaders would actually solve real problems, do you know what would happen? They would get re-elected, keep their positions and gain mass amount of accolades. But so many of your leaders fail to realize this very basic, fundamental aspect of leadership. When you take care of the ones you are suppose to take care of, you stay where you are…

To dominate the <u>Physical-side</u> of life on your Planet, become really good at these simple, yet fundamental aspects of being an A-type Advanced Species.

Of course the overall potential of the Physical-side of life on Earth is heavily dependent on the Mental-side. The Mental-side (Metaphysical) is the lowest hole in the bucket for the Human Species.

<u>**1. Re-imagining Earth's Economy:**</u> First, imagine what life would be on Earth if the stress of money did not exist. What would Humans become if they were not restricted by "The Economy"? Would Humans become more peaceful or more violent if the stress of money was diminished? Would crime increase or decrease? How many less deaths would Earth have if the stress of money was drastically reduced? Would it be safer or more dangerous where you live if the stresses of money were eliminated or reduced?

We, on our Planet, had to at least try something different. Even if what we tried failed, we had to try. If it failed, we could always go back to how it was. But at least we would now know if something different was better or worse for us.

We had to look at our Economy different. We were curious to see what would happen to our species and our Planet when we took away the stresses of money for ALL members of our species.

Our first adjustment; to radically change the way we perceived money and our economy. If we created money and the economy and they were not driven and governed by the Laws of Nature; we could then let our imaginations run wild and free in creating something different, equal, efficient, and based on common-sense.

We decided that our Advanced Species would never be held back by something that we have full control over. Money is made-up. The Economy is made-up. If it does not work, then make it up again.

Choosing life-decisions based less on money and more on common-sense long-term vision will allow you to pass up the majority of Humans.

This is a few examples of what we did. (You can try any or all of them. Remember, if something doesn't work, you can always go back to the way it used to be.)

1. Everyone after they turn a certain age gets a monthly Planetary Income until they die. It's enough to pay for one's housing, food, and basic utilities. If we want to be a dominant A-type Species, we had to eliminate the very problems and stresses that our species created. No more species-created homelessness, no more starving, no more losing basic needs (water, electricity) etc… If someone became poor or homeless or is starving because of their own stupidity, that's on them. We can't fix stupid. Some individuals will fail no matter how much you help them. We let them fail. We had to decide to move on and not coddle

everyone. We decided that if any individual failed it would be because of their own personal decisions, not because of the economy that our species created. We created an economy that took care of all of our basic fundamental needs and securities. We took away the fear of not having a home. We took away the fear of not having water or electricity. We took away the stress of not having enough money to feed our families. If one still fails after all that, its on them.

2. We created and/or expanded <u>Purposeful Jobs</u>. We paid people much more if they held jobs that made our species and/or Planet better. Since the economy and money was imagined by us, we decided to imagine what would happen if we paid people high salaries to help maintain, manage, and clean up our Planet.

But first, we paid people more in certain critical fundamental areas that were already established. Which areas could we recruit the most open-minded, adaptable, diversely-intelligent people who would make the most difference in rebuilding our Planet and species?

Teaching of the young of our species became a top profession. We wanted our top individuals making the most difference in the critical developmental years of our children. We wanted to create problem-solvers, not problem-creators. All teachers on our Planet became some of the highest paid after that. Properly educating/teaching an Advanced Species' young will bring an enormous amount of long-term benefits. We pay the best to produce the best.

Planetary Jobs. Then we thought about paying high salaries to other areas of our Planet where we had the most urgent needs now while also helping us in the future.

We figured that since our actions on our Planet were causing some undesired Climate Change, we probably should start looking for ways to reduce that. Our Planet had much of the same problems that Earth has now. We thought about the History of our Planet much like yours. Our Planet, much like yours, has gone through several catastrophic events that devastated life where an enormous amount of species were lost. But each time these events happened, our Planet and your Planet has come back and flourished. We realized that it came back from near death to lots of life without us being there.

Same as your Planet. Earth has suffered extensive loss of life throughout its existence. But each time its come back. But you shouldn't and don't have to fix it alone. You have creatures on your Planet that have rebuilt it from near nothing multiple times. Use them to help you fix the problems that you have created. Never underestimate the power of plants and insects and all the other critters. They have, before Humans ever existed, rebuilt and re-balanced Planet Earth multiple times following Mass Extinctions and Globally-catastrophic disasters.

For us, we let many of the neglected and damaged areas of our Planet return naturally to how it used to be before we altered it. We simply let Nature do its thing while we manage and enhance it. We worked to achieve high diversity of life in as many areas as we possibility could squeeze them into on our Planet. The more living relationships we allowed to rebuild and interconnect within our ecosystems allowed us to rebuild our Planet to a much healthier state.

We wanted more diversity on our Planet. We wanted more diversity of wild, native plants growing where they should be growing. We wanted the large diversity of plants to bring back the large diversity of insects we once had. So we managed for diversity of life, not profit. Actually, we came up with programs that paid people very well who naturally increased biodiversity of wildlife on land they owned or managed. We fined people who decreased biodiversity on the land that they owned or managed. We made intelligent long-term decisions based on the good of our Planet along with our entire species and all other species, not based on how much money we can make from this or from that.

We also reduced our Global use of substances that were foreign to our billions-year-old Planet. If any substance we created was made against the Natural Laws of Nature, it was highly reduced in usage. We felt that our Planet, like Earth, has been forming these deeply-connected relationships between and within the chemical world of life. Meaning for billions of years on our Planet as well as Earth; forests, oceans, rivers, prairies, soils etc, and all the living things living within them, and all the tiniest of chemical reactions within all of everything, have been developing and evolving together naturally. If we use substances, *whether we made them or not*, that disrupts that highly important chemical relationship within living systems, we either don't use it or we save it for rare occasions. It takes us and our Planet that much longer to re-heal itself if we keep putting foreign substances into our soils and waters that our Planet doesn't recognize.

Our way of growing our food changed. The way we viewed our soils and waters changed. The days of growing one type of food on hundreds, thousands, or millions of acres of land were now gone. We emphasized high degrees of biodiversity wherever we could. We continued to grow our own food but we gave much of our farmed land back to Nature. We intellectually intertwined growing our food within the Nature found on our Planet. We expanded our Forests along with growing food throughout them. Simply put, we stopped destroying millions of acres of highly beneficial, highly diverse forests along with their respective soils, to replace them with a very few crops. But we did not give up growing our food. We just adapted and changed the way we did it.

That's what's so great about being an A/B-type Advanced Species. We can keep what we have now, plus gain much much more, all the while being able to healthily maintain ourselves and our Planet.

For us, it wasn't about what we would have to give up to save our Planet. It was about what we could do to rebuild and re-strengthen our Planet to high enough levels so that we did not have to give up those things we wanted to keep. A healthy Planet can fix many problems before they get worse and can allow you to have more of the things you want to keep.

Paying ourselves to fix our Planet's problems that we created. So we thought it would be tremendously beneficial to our Planet and our species to pay people very well who took care of our Planet.

We created many high-paying jobs that put many of us working within our Forests, our Oceans, our Lakes, our Deserts, our Rainforests, our Rivers, our Grasslands etc … These jobs allowed us to pay people to maintain, clean, and manage our Planet forever. These jobs will never go away. The long-term benefits to our species and our Planet were simply too great to ever give this up.

We also paid people very well who had skills in recycling, re-building, and re-using. The more we could re-use, the less waste we had. Less waste, less time spent on waste.

We also created hybrid jobs that allowed people to work part of their time in our cities and part of their time in Nature. The subtle and not-so-subtle benefits that would eventually come out of this type of work was incredible. There was a monumental drop in both mental-health and physical-health problems.

1. We virtually eliminated daily monetary stresses by creating a Global Income.
2. Individuals are allowed to make a really good income *on top of* the Global Income working outside rebuilding and giving back to the very Planet that created them. **Purpose driven careers.**
3. Working and interacting with Nature greatly diminishes mental stress. Species mental-health increases.
4. Working and interacting with Nature keeps the body moving which also greatly improves physical health. Species physical-health increases.
5. By allowing our individuals to work on many different areas throughout consecutive years, their brains are further developed. We allow ourselves to complete long-term multi-year projects in a variety of areas (forests, oceans, rivers etc). This allows anyone who works on these areas to see the change and outcome that their work has allowed. Increased ability to connect past, present, and future events occurs. Further individual brain development occurs. Further development of the Advanced Species.
6. We also paid big businesses, corporations to assist clean-up and to create massive amounts of biodiversity. We allowed businesses and corporations to exist only if they cleaned up after themselves and either left the areas they used at least as equally healthy as it was before they used it or more healthy. The more healthy they made it after they used it brought them even more money. So any business or

corporation could make just as much money by improving the Earth. Some of our biggest businesses became some of the biggest rebuilders of our Planet. People on Earth love money. Make that work for your Planet.

We also shut down or heavily fined any businesses or corporations that caused more damage that we would have to clean-up and fix. We don't mind paying them to clean up and fixing the Planet but we will no longer tolerate unnecessary, time-wasting Planet-damaging types of businesses. Each business has the option to either clean up after itself or be eliminated.

By creating these Forever-Planet-Maintenance careers; we have found a way to maintain, clean, and manage our Planet. This has also allowed for us to attain high levels of species physical and mental health.

In Summary:

If Humans can conquer the following mental and physical aspects of life on Planet Earth, then they can accomplish what no other species has or may ever be able to accomplish in the History of our Universe.

Mental:
1. Equality (you are failing here)
2. Open-Mindedness (you are failing here)
3. Imagination (you are not failing here but not succeeding enough either)
4. Long-Term Vision (you are failing here)
5. Parenting/Child-development (you are failing here)

Physical:
1. Planet Maintenance (you are failing here)
2. Planet Management (you are failing here)
3. Pollution Control (you are failing here)
4. Technology (you are good here)
5. Information (you are good here)
6. Re-writing the Global Economy into something that unleashes the Human Brain. Humans need to create an economy that enhances the Human spirit, not one that diminishes it. (you are failing here)
7. Developing a Planetary Monthly Income that drastically reduces Global crimes, starvation, abuse, neglect, poverty, unemployment, homelessness… etc… etc… etc… (you haven't tried this one yet but you should)
8. Developing purposeful Planetary Careers that solve multiple Human and Earth problems. (you are failing here)
9. Throw a Global Party every 4 years celebrating the hard work your Species has done in recovering your Planet. The Planet parties together! (we can't wait for you to be here)

Modern Humans living on Earth right now in 2020 find themselves at a pivotal point in their existence. In your current direction of development, we believe that you are choosing the path that leads to more chaos and more problems. The current Human-decision-making process revolves around what's good for the individual, not what's good for the entire species or your Planet.

You are headed for the dreaded and highly dangerous Narcissistic Era of an Advanced Species existence. Actually, we believe you are already in the beginning of it. This Era is where individuals believe their beliefs, needs, and desires are more important than anyone or anything else's. They also believe their beliefs, needs, and desires are more important than their very own Planet and all the other species living on it. Most of these types of individuals are developed from the very environment that they were developed in, they are usually not genetic-anomalies.

Once modern Humans realize that its not too late to adjust their toxic behavior, they can avoid going further into the Narcissistic Era. The other path that's opposite to the Narcissistic Era is what we did on our Planet. We have described much of that path throughout our writings and analysis of your species.

We wish Humans on Earth the best of luck. This is it, this is the time. Can you take advantage of the very rare opportunity that lies waiting in front of you? We hope so. Like we stated earlier, we believe the Human brain is the most powerful living thing in the Universe. We also believe that Earth is one of the most perfect Planets throughout the entire Universe.

So what do you get when you combine a maximized, powerful Human brain with a dynamically diverse, optimally healthy Planet?

No one knows. No one in your position has ever done it. Mostly because no has been in your position. How many Advanced Species are out there that have what you have? Global communication and connection, information, technology, knowledge, inventions, a nearly perfect Planet, many past failures and mistakes to learn from…

Can modern Humans on Earth seize this rare opportunity presented to them at this time or will they waste it?

$\longrightarrow$

What can I do as an individual Human do to help our species and our Planet? *This is the question I asked myself continually over the last few years.*

There are plenty of effective things that one could do and continually work on to prevent from becoming the type of Human that one doesn't want to become.

1. Develop a more powerful Human mind and brain that allows you to withstand Inequality and Injustice. (Extensively discussed in Chapters 1-3 in <u>Turtle</u>)

2. Develop a more powerful independently-thinking Human mind and brain that allows you to stand up to

others who keep you down. (Extensively discussed in Chapters 1-3 in <u>Turtle</u>)

3. Resist your desire to tell others how to live their life. The internal stress that accumulates within you, while trying to control and telling others how to live their life; is one of the most dangerous things one can do to themselves. You will gain so much internal freedom and release of stress if you just don't care how others live their life. (Extensively discussed in Chapter 5 in <u>Turtle</u>)

4. Continue learning a wide variety of skills throughout your life, even for a few minutes here and there. Successful Humans are not stuck in one or two careers. Keep learning and keep adapting. It will help to build a powerful brain. (Extensively discussed in Chapter 4 in <u>Turtle</u>)

5. Become a dynamic parent/mentor/influencer of kids. This also helps to build a very strong Human brain. (Extensively discussed in Chapter 6 in <u>Turtle</u>)

6. Start learning the basic fundamentals of how the natural living systems (forests, oceans, ponds, deserts etc) work around you. Earth will need plenty of us to help her out. The more people we have that understand the basic fundamental aspects of how our natural world works benefits all of us. This also further develops the Human brain in many deep ways. (Discussed in various depths throughout the book)

7. Develop the weak side of your brain. If you are more of a left-brained science/analytical type, then continually work to build your right-brained creative side. The opposite is also true. Those who continually build both sides of their brains are continually smarter

than those who don't. (Discussed in various depths throughout the book)

8. If you have money and/or land and are wondering what you can do with it to benefit our species, other species, and/or our Planet, try this.

1. Buy, acquire, or manage land if you don't have any. Buy any kind of land, the cheapest, the neglected, the abused, whatever.
2. Allow it to convert itself back to its original state (before Humans altered it) as naturally as possible. The less use of foreign, non-natural substances, the better.
3. While letting your land grow wild and free, start learning the fundamentals of how to effectively create a biodiverse, healthy piece of Earth.
4. Unbiasedly observe what looks healthy versus unhealthy to us and other species. When you look at a piece of land, think of how many different species could live there or not live there. Would they be healthy living there or not? Continue to watch and learn what makes some areas more or less productive in regards to supporting a wide variety of life. You will be surprised how quickly you will learn how to recognize unproductive land versus productive land. You will also quickly begin to see which Human practices are making high diversity of life better or worse.

Start here:
A. Since high biodiversity (Lots of different living things) is our goal on Earth, we can simply manage for that, without knowing much about plants or land at first. Look at your property. What do you see? How many different types of plant do you see? How many different types of heights of plants do you see? How much sunlight does your property receive and in what areas?

B. Create and maintain high levels of biodiversity and watch the potential of your land explode. If you see too much of one kind, even if that one kind is good, you most likely have to reduce them. We want more of different types of plants, not more of the same. We want to see a good balance of different kinds of plants that have many different heights and shapes that can support a wide variety of other living things. Short plants feed and support different animals than medium or tall plants.

C. Consistently assist your land as it rebuilds and heals itself. Land (forests, prairies, etc) have been building and rebuilding and healing themselves for long periods of time. However, we as Humans, can further assist them. We can help to remove invasive species that causes more harm than good. We can help maintain the balance of high diversity of life.

There are few things that any Human can do that will benefit the Planet more than helping to maintain its high level of productivity and biodiversity. It is and will always be one of the most important careers/aspirations on Earth.

I thoroughly believe that Humans and the Human brain, today on Earth, have what it takes to turn things around...

Notes:

Notes:

Lightning Source UK Ltd.
Milton Keynes UK
UKHW021404120620
364900UK00009B/510